# THE CALL OF THE UNWRITTEN

# THE CALL OF THE UNWRITTEN

*Poems by* Adrian G R Scott

Copyright 2010 Adrian G R Scott

Sheffield, England

ISBN 978-1-4461-3806-9

*For Wilma*

*Tu sei la mia musa*

You must learn one thing:
the world was made to be free in.

DAVID WHYTE<br>*Sweet Darkness*

# PREFACE

As someone who has always written poetry but only over the last two years dedicated serious time and energy to becoming a poet, I have been prey to many of the blights that beset the new shoots of creativity. I have tried to eradicate the habit of being overly florid in my language, tumbling adjectives together, and writing showy sentences – I am doing it now – or going to the other extreme and writing in such an opaque way that even I am bemused when I return to it.

Some of these poems were originally written over the last twenty-five years and have been somewhat reworked over the past few months. The rest are the fruit of early rising to write before the business of the day gets going. This is my first attempt at publishing a collection, and I am grateful to those who have offered critique and reaction to my lines. It is painful to admit that a poem you have given birth to with long labour still falls short of the honest craft you aimed for. Yet it is a great joy to incorporate another's comments and see the work smoothed out and more ready for the rough world.

In putting together a collection, one tries to bring all the work up to a level that is consistent with the skill one has acquired. However I have allowed some of the poems to retain the naïveté of my earlier years, as they are milestones in my story. This has been a major motivation for publishing this collection: to tell my story in a way that will resonate with you, the reader. So it is with trepidation and no little joy that I offer these poems in the hope that it will step across the boundary from my small world into yours and carry you more deeply into the great story we are all part of.

Glen Mount<br>
Sheffield<br>
May 2010

# Contents

|  | *Page* |
|---|---|
| Preface | ix |
| Taking Stock | 1 |
| A Secret Salvation | 2 |
| From the Medals of My Father | 4 |
| The Stag on My Road | 6 |
| Keel Hauled | 8 |
| A Poem of Grudging Self-Acceptance | 10 |
| Writing Poems | 14 |
| The Golden Thread | 16 |
| Self Portrait as an Idealist – Age 27 | 18 |
| Dandelions | 19 |
| Meeting My Father-in-Law | 21 |
| That Night in Paris | 23 |
| A Rite of Passage | 25 |
| The Origins of Fire | 28 |
| The Uses of Water | 30 |
| Moon Madness | 33 |
| After Christmas | 35 |
| I Heard One Night | 36 |
| Walking with My Wife | 37 |
| The Call of the Unwritten | 38 |
| The Relics of Saint Therese | 39 |
| Jung Said | 40 |
| Emmaus | 41 |

| | |
|---|---|
| An Unexpected Passion | 43 |
| Song of a Motherless Son | 45 |
| The Boy Within | 47 |
| Brief Beauty | 49 |
| Disconsolation | 51 |
| Last Rites | 52 |
| The Chair Maker Cycle | 53 |
| Inconsequence and Silence | 57 |
| There Is One Thing Necessary | 58 |
| Gabriel | 60 |
| The Raven-Haired Woman | 62 |
| The Circles of Women | 64 |
| The Rook and the Hawk | 67 |
| Frontier Dream | 68 |
| The Pillowed State | 71 |
| What My Migraines Taught Me | 72 |
| A Poem for My Children | 74 |
| Warts of Wisdom | 77 |
| The Curriculum of Winter | 78 |
| The Real Truth | 79 |
| The Needle on the Don | 81 |
| No Such Thing as Right or Wrong | 84 |
| The Georgia O'Keefe Museum | 86 |

# Taking Stock

How would it feel
if, out of the
darkening grey of
dusk-fall
clouds as they
lower themselves
on to the backs
of the hills,
an unseen hand
reached down
and removed,
at a stroke,
everything
that makes up the
minutes of your
life and left you in
the stripped yearning
of a bare night? And
then in the cold
initiatory shiver of
a new dawn, that
same hand returned
your life to you in
discrete items, like
clothing on hangers
and shoes in boxes?
What would you
choose to keep for
that expedition
we call our life, and
more important,
what, finally
would you choose
to leave behind?

# A Secret Salvation

Monday morning wet
in the window-framed garden,
a new pup sleeps on my shoulder,
her nose on my thoughts, as I
tap away on a laptop, iPod
playing, an evolving poet.

Debussy hovers over the keyboard
as I try to craft honest lines.
I open the window and my
thoughts escape up to the dark peak
and the snake's pass, where
Kinder Scout receives the clouds'
grace with limestone joy. Waters
run to the valley where my
house perches as a heron rises up
spreading his wings against the
ruined works where men ground iron.

The pup stirs, the track changes,
the swan's lake trembles with violins
as a single oboe sweeps a curved
neck's slender whiteness towards the city,
where horns blare at the commuters.

Meanwhile, in my little garret
the music ends, leaving a silence brushed
with the edges of birdsong. Now audible,
the clock marks time and motion,
the grafter's mockery of the unproductive
writer. Poets - what use are they when
proper folk grapple with the hard world?

But poetry is a pension fund against
the stealthy loss, that wakes you
in the dark demanding, 'What are you here for?'

So in that same darkness I pull
myself apart and in this morning
attempt to give form to things
unspeakable, to record the speckles
of birdsong, with a poet's faith
that this Monday morning has a
secret salvation - if only I could write it.

# From the Medals of My Father

From the sale of my late father's medals
I bought a book of Pasternak's poems, in which
is recorded all our sorrow as now
I mouth the words death stole from you.
The symbols of victory and defeat
that emblazoned your breast, long forgotten,
recur in images that prickle like spines.
Remembering you pulls reluctantly
a plaster from an unhealed wound, and as
the warm blood forms bright, domed droplets,
lurking pain is as sleepless as my nights.
Father, why have you forsaken me?

I once recall seeing a strange fish,
whose healing secretions were only released
when it sensed affliction in its offspring;
I hope it was a dream of you and me.
Father, why have you forsaken me?

Aged eleven, I went on holiday,
left you in good health. Then something
awful on my Grandmothers lips: he is dead.
She and her sister walked me through
fields of sugar beet, sweet anesthetists,
then they let me be. Too complacent, I never
said goodbye; now our parting has sculpted my life.
Father, why have you forsaken me?

Months after, I caught sight of you framed
in the door, but the light played charlatan,
left me the house empty, bereft of it and you.
Father, why have you forsaken me?

Death drove a wedge to part us;
that wedge now props the door open,
which seemed shut and bolted darkness.
Yet the poems still speak of our parting.
No continuity, just a tortuous gap,
a stretch of fallow soil. Loss
is the water that splits the seeds open,
goading me to grow up to you. Grief is
the nurse that takes my temperature, and
as I drain the cup you poured for me,
its emptiness is a painful preface.

My Mother sold your medals to forget
the past; I bought the poems to rescue it.

# The Stag on My Road

Crossing the Yorkshire
Wolds on the way
to Whitby, a stop for relief
on a single track road.
Stepping down
to find a spot as
before me spreads a
sea of wheat, all green ears
whispering, turning gold.
About to return to the road, I stop,
rapt in the swaying field. Then

a swishing to the left
as panoramic past me
strides a young stag just
sprouting antlers from his
beautiful brow, definite
in his direction, a prow
through a wheaten sea.
I gasp with delight
as he leaves me standing,
his tan sleekness,
outbreaking wildness
from a rural earth. 'Where

are you going,' I call
to his retreating rear. 'Come
and see' is the whispered
reply from corn and deer.
But what am I, clod man
of earth with a need to pee?
Yet the vision is mine,

a sacrilege to flee,
tracking his deering course
to what horizon will I be
led? Better to go after him
than to die in bed.

# Keel Hauled

If you haven't been
keel hauled by life,
then you're not living.
You have been
getting the message
all your life, the
ascent of spring,
the long dark of winter.

Yet for many it is
hidden in plain sight.
Your ordinary life is a
drama, wearing the
masks you see at the
theatre: weeping and
laughing, exits and
entrances, tragedy
and comedy. Then
there is the hot leap
of love and the
blunt fact of death.

The key is to remain
in touch with your
soul – and by soul
I mean the sense
that you are here
for a reason, that
you are meant to
be alive. That there
is a you, a river bed
to the daily flood

that just is. So as
you walk past the
shop windows
mirroring glimpses
of your true defeats,
welcome their hunger
to be recast into your life,
to make of you a human.

**Keelhauling**: The sailor was tied to a rope that looped beneath the vessel, thrown overboard on one side of the ship, and dragged under the ship's keel to the other side.
– *Wikipedia*

# A Poem of Grudging Self-Acceptance

I hear my voice on a
recording and cringe: the
flat vowels, the lack of bass
notes, the overall effect
of a dim northerner appalls me.
I know Hockney and Bennett
have made the Yorkshire
accent credible, but they hail
from the more well-heeled
parts like Leeds and Harrogate,
the places where the BBC make
*Look North* and from whence
came the assured silk
hats of Bradford millionaires.

I come from the steel-worked,
Coal-mined, rougher-edged
southern end of the county.
Sheffield, city equated with
grime and muck, the location
for *The Full Monty*, where men
had their work stripped from them,
so they went the whole hog
and took off their clothes for
money instead. The bluff,
well-scrubbed, working-class
face of Brian Glover came
from Sheffield; he played the
vicious sports teacher in *Kes*,
another film that showed
our true colours: the grey
brown domain of pits and pain,
crucibles and winding gear.

Being bred in South Yorkshire
was like putting on an overcoat
that I began to grow into
at my first football match,
Man United against Sheffield
Wednesday (five–four to us and
seventy thousand men moving
and jeering, reeking of cigarettes
and Bovril). I was given the run of the
place as a kid, tuppence to anywhere
on our brown and cream buses
till we were deregulated. My
reception teacher told me
there was no *r* in bath, so say it
right, lad. Born in London with a
mother from Willesden, I had to fit
myself to a northern idiom, a
place where we mash our tea,
a place I grudgingly and
gratefully accept has reared me.

I have come to love this town
with its sibilant Stannington and
Shire Green, the earthy romance
of Rivelin and Dungworth, as I declare
her common beauty. The view
of the world she has given me is not
flat like my vowels but riven by
seven rivers through seven hills, with valleys
that cut deep into the heart of things,
that taught us to make cutlery and silver.

We are an accumulation of villages
punctuated by civic parks narrating
a homely tale, where you expect
to greet a friend on the street, where
we call each other 'love'. The nature
of these folk is one of cheerful
ordinariness, the flat-capped celebrants
of cobbled streets and the pinnied
mothers who kept the front room for best.

But what are we coming to now,
Sheffield and me? We have cleared
away the industrial debris and made
of it Meadowhall; we even have a
winter garden. What has become
of the common people in this
age of texts and freeview?
Will call-centres and supermarkets
offer the self-respect that our knives and
forks in the hands of the world did?

We are building loft apartments and
welcoming students, but where is our
soul? We are still at the ragged end
of our past and don't quite know
how to step into the future. It
had better not be with big ideas,
with projects that cost an arm and
a leg; we already have enough white
elephants wandering our sloping
streets. Once we hauled gritstone
wheels down from the moors to

grind our steel into beauty. We
should to talk to each other at bus
stops and in shops about what can
be shined and sharpened today.

To tell each other new stories and
in the telling rescue the worn
things we still need and colloquially
create the new hallmarks that read
'Made in Sheffield'. So I will listen
to your voices, overhear your
chatter and your stillness; I will
speak out about my city in my
ready northern tongue and make a
simple solid vow to tell your stories
with the honesty I got from you.

# Writing Poems

To boil down
to its essential core
the image you
were born with –
that is a hard calling.
To take the off cuts
of a life and reduce
them for hours
on a green stove
with stainless steel
hobs. To end
up with ivory
smooth bones
that sit neatly in
the palm of the
writer's calloused
hand. To confront the
harsh white page
even when your
own unruly black
letters induce
a daily dying.
Crossing and
recrossing the
doorsill of failure.
That precarious
emptiness whose
other side is
only reached by
sticking with the
metaphor until
it stands on its

own feet and
answers you
back. Once this
erosion has
occurred, the
smooth naked
bones can be
threaded along
a narrative of
reduction,
to wear away
the crusted
carapace of the
insulated heart.
Of the soul that
has lost the vision
of common wonder,
dulled by
mundane misanthropies,
deadened by
monotonous media
only to be
illumined
by the poem's
beads threading
through
the fingers
of the mind,
framing mantras
of sweet awareness
to the beauty
of this ordinary life.

# The Golden Thread

I first found
the golden thread when
Father Christmas gave me a book of the
Famous Five; I was six and I haven't stopped reading
since.

If you follow
this thread of life,
it will inevitably wind itself
around its dark, foreboding twin.

In this vein
the famous five
went to Smuggler's Top
and met a dark-haired boy called
Sooty Lenoir and his sister, Marybelle.

Beauty and
the beast. he said, but
in this life both are your friends.

Life's adventure,
like the chapters in my book,
will have puzzling things and strange
happenings, curious discoveries, and a rescuing dog.

The children
in the story had
to go through the hill –
not round it or over it, but through it.
The worst you can do is ignore the hill.

As a boy
I entered two
worlds: the realm
of books and the belly
of a beast named loss;
each gave birth to the adult.

Jesus used
grown-up language
for it: he spoke of a sign:
reluctant Jonah's great-bellied fish.

Now, I like
books on deserts; one
said that bewilderment
occasions a different way of knowing.

Whatever your
life is like, know
that the golden thread
is always entwined around
its inky sibling, but my first
book still says things come right at last.

# Self Portrait as an Idealist – Age 27
## (After Vincent)

Hope's adrenaline triggers my living,
a welding torch fusing vision and despair,
a tongue to dumbness, night into day. As
my vocal chords twang and snap, string by
string, other throats will catch the note – new voices,
too many candles to be snuffed out. Death
is the loud hailer who announces change as
I gamble my cowardice against blinkered
indifference. One a gust-blown tree,
the other a veneer. I know my self-inflicted
wounds give me the look of a fool, but fools
have kept kings sane; clowns' pale white faces weep
tears that can scald sense on the skin of history.
As to my palate I add blue and yellow
to sing of the sun's flower in the night sky.

# Dandelions

Long before those
showy spring delicates,
the Lupines and Delphiniums,
are any more than shoots
for slug and snail to chew,
the anarchists of the plant
realm are up and ready
to bloom. Those yellow-headed
punks with spiky hair
that quickly peroxides white.
Their seeds follicled into the
spongy scalp that balds to
a stream of flying stars constellating
the next boundless generation.

No amount of toxic compound
can eradicate these
anarchic collectives
with their callous disregard
for law and ordered lawns.
They have even
persuaded children
to play at telling time,
wafting their seeds to
the whipping wind. Such
power in the dandelion,
to reflect the returning
sun and question our
compulsion to control
when we, like them, were
made for wildness and abandon.

There is a story
of weeds and wheat
in which only the
moss-encrusted God sees
the destiny of nature.
It is our gaze, not our hand,
that germinates such appreciation.
How savage to yank out their
yellow heads in a sacrilege of order.

# Meeting My Father-in-Law

Your warm and bearlike hand
grasped my slim, collegiate palm
more turned to turning pages than
industry and grind. At this first
meeting you greeted me with a
gruff Glaswegian growl, warm with
challenge,

'Come with me, son,'
as I was driven off to view your
hard and grafted empire. I tried
to enter the conversation with
the man of worth, a row of lorries
at his back.

'You should write a book,'
I spouted, 'be a business guru.'
'The only ones writing fucking books
are going fucking bust.'
Words voiced in working-class granite.

'What are you qualified in?'
you asked in search of succour for
a daughter. 'Theology,' I squeaked,
the sumptuous leather seat expanding,
making me a boy again. Your blank
incomprehension travelled soundlessly
over this revelation with the
smoothness of well-treaded tires.

'Where are you family,' you segued
through our differences. My father
died as had yours, mine at eleven

and yours at only eight, both boys asked
too early to be men.
'Your Mother?' 'We speak every day,'
I managed. You nodded as you showed
me yards of trucks, your name
emblazoned over every one.

That day we made a contract
of incredulity, two worlds linked by a
boyhood loss and the robust love
of a mother. So when I came to you in
your final coffin and took that cold yet
once warm hand, I knew the fulfillment
of a kept, unspoken vow. Both to spend
the last living breath on a work that
beats the grave and builds a column's
base on which is carved; here I stand
so my family can travel on in grace.

# That Night in Paris

That night in Paris
you travelled a great
distance to arrive,
descending from
your solitary realm.

Your raven hair and
sleek body enfolding my
unsteady boyhood.
Hovering at the doorsill
of consummation yet
with passionate chastity
espousing a promise
of fulfillment.

A panic inundated you
in the French streets
about our engagement
as we traipsed the artists'
quarter, lighting candles in
the Sacre Coeur. To embrace
me would breach your seclusion
and disclose you to another.

I told you in my arrogance
you would never find
a better spouse for your
singular soul. Still the
shadow of Notre Dame
conjured rejection,
that crouching gargoyle
of humpbacked fear.

But you found some
inner recess in that
unvoiced night of passion
and danced out to
touch my naked soul
with fragile, translucent wings.

I did not recognize then
you would be an echo
of my intimate Eve and
I would come to mirror
your secret, shining Adam.

# A Rite of Passage

I climb the promontory, silent peninsula
Above the plains to the shaman's circle.
The belly of God, umbilical, fertile,
Fecund, swelling, the womb of God.
My belly is His, His belly is mine;
God has eaten me and I have eaten God.
I have drunk the tears of God,
Tears of grief and pain, woe begotten.
I have ground the pain of God,
And God has pained the ground of me.
God has split, fractured, and broken,
I am cut, gashed, a cracked pot.
I am nothing and no one, soon gone;
God is everyone and everything.
I am encircled by God, circling God
I encompass God, little clod God.
I am a horn of desire, hard,
I want to enseed the world.
I am a comfort to the earth;
In my arms I feel its hurt and rape.
The earth has been fucked
By bastard men with no hearts.
I am purple balm in Israel,
Soft oil and pure ointment.
I am Adam's flesh and bone, failed,
With moisture, tears for the stones.
I am a cocooned infant, enwombed,
Cramped in groaning limbo.
Then I am hanging, pulled out,
As lightening arcs from sky to lake.
Satan has fallen, rumbling down
Plague to earth, brazen, crass.

No, listen, God is coming, in the
Thunderheads, awesome and growling.
God is the fearsome shaman,
His bullroarer makes the ground shake!
What difference does this little-shit life
Make to the God of the thunder crack?
Yet I carry lightening in my scrotum,
Swimming seed that gives new life.
God is here and his coming scares me;
He is scouring and scraping, scarring me,
Hailstones like pebbles on my back,
Pounding on my spine and head.
The wooden crucifix I set up, crashed
to earth behind me, crossly smashed.
His limbs splintered, scattering,
Like so many sparks in the stubble.
His peace arches over me, caressing me,
Yet this pinioning is no passive state.
He is the arrow of God, to pierce the flint hearted.
He tells me the secret of the shaman,
It is this – the shaman knows nothing!
I wait for more – a gulf of quiet,
A brooding of thunderous silence.
The shaman has virginal mind, pierced and
Penetrated, possessed by wounded innocence,
Both novice and initiate,
But always the disciple's tongue.
This is the shaman's call:
Loss that is all gain.
In my open hands a stone,
The earth has given me a gift.
It is a rib, a part of herself,

a rounded gritstone sacrament
To hold as a remembering until
I die, to carry with reverencing.
Thunder; again God is here,
Crashing over me, breathing fire.
Fear curdles my insides, death is here,
I am alone before its luminosity.
Then the storm passes by, and
In its wake is left only the son of earth.
Silently standing over me, gazing
Down on me, he enters me.
He is the beloved Son and so am I.
His blood courses through my veins,
His presence mine and mine is his.
A circle of elders move around me
Blessing way chants, and cloaks on my shoulders.

*Ghost Ranch, New Mexico,* 2002

# The Origins of Fire
(a poem for men)

The origins of fire
are hidden in the dark,
secret place where our
ancestors stole fire from
the gods. This incendiary
power can ignite the green
fuse in our genes, molecular
strands of memory thrusting
us out into the elemental
solitude of our state.

I have never known a man
who doesn't test the ashes
of last night's fire to gauge
the chances of reignition.

When a man has expended
the fires of youth and
spent the fuel of innocence,
when he has entered the
age of dust and ashes, he
is heir to the dissolving
tears of grief.

This is no easy passage,
many will try to frighten
you with brimstone and
burning, but I say to you
that hell is not a destination;
it is the subway of the
burnt ones. It is the blazing

of those who are holy,
holes scorched into the fabric
of the ego, holes we can trust.

This is the true fire of
wounded brotherhood, of
breathtaking together, of
birthing a wisdom from the
embers of each day's burning,
to fan to flame the sparks,
fire for the earth – and how I
wish it were burning already.

# The Uses of Water

The scouring of salt
in seawater can be
caustic and cathartic:
moon-pulled waves offering
their rhythmic invitation
to enter aching
deserts of ocean wildness,
an invitation that
to voyage is to be.

But the silken tensile surface
of freshwater broken
by my naked body slipping
into the lake is sensual,
a virginal moment,
ripe for harvesting.
This is the plunge into soul,
where dark angels lurk
in the reed beds.
An eel touched me once
and left a slime trail on my
ribcage near to my heart.

I once leaned back into
the spring waters
of a white lady with a
blue sash, lowered by old
French men in Lourdes,
icy spring water enveloping
my backward falling body
in a freezing fatal embrace,
then hauling me up

into the world of shivering
originality, my senses jangling,
my skin gilded.

Again in intensive care
I used hospital
water to baptise
a grape-choked child,
its pouring sending
her silently flowing
out of the room.
The mother told me that
her man wasn't speaking.
I said that perhaps
there was nothing to say.
He looked at me as if I had
offered his drowning a lifebelt.
The water in their eyes
overflowed into mine.

Now we bottle water as
if it was a commodity,
but the plastic
will run out with the oil,
and we will have to cup
our hands to the rain again
and give freely to the stranger.

I read of a desert planet
where a messiah changed the
tears of death into the water
of life; isn't that

what messiahs are for?
We will all be messiahs
when we submit
to the humbling fact
that we are mainly water,
that we can be undammed,
that we sink or swim together.

# Moon Madness

It does not take
Armstrong's small
step for a man
or his giant leap to
apprehend the moon.
It takes twenty-eight days
of waxing and waning,
of tides and menstrual blood.
Whoever said that colonising
was the way to gain knowledge
of a thing? Twenty-eight
dreaming nights where
every part of the dream
is you. After all, there is
only so much to be learned
from the evenness of sunlight.
Wolves howl at the moon;
humans become wolves and
bite each other when they
have been tamed too long.
The lunatic was the
original moonwalker,
wild enough to
rage and weep in the
sleepiness of night.
But I say we are mad
to think of life as a
line of progress
and that poles are to be
shunned in favour
of a false equator. Take
a month of yourself and

speak it out loud, on the
new moon in a sacred circle,
and I promise you that
the secreted self that lurks
in the dark will emerge
with good intent. Then as
she waxes, the unearthly
silver of the rising moon
will illustrate so much
more of you than
daylight can reveal.

# After Christmas

Holiday keeps the world at bay,
cossets, comforts each quiet day.
A safe house, Yule log warming,
the easy Christmas yawning.
Now a new term, waking under dawn,
hearing the dark morning's scorn.
Calling, 'Please, what is my calling
and whose burdens am I hauling?'
Time to look at the faded year
to be candid, direct, and clear.
I have been trading myself,
my precious animating health,
for a work of worthy deeds
in the name of other's needs.
If I am to serve the tender fire
and rouse my dormant desire,
I need to live from the inside,
to serenely, firmly brush aside
the tyrannical phone's demand,
to be the work of a gentler hand.
Not swirl the whirl of other's schemes,
but rather live my given dreams.

# I Heard One Night

I heard one night
that God was coming.
I rose the next day
with great anticipation.
I put on my best clothes,
my finest shoes and
cut my finger nails.
My family wished me well
and sent me on my way.
I went first to the church,
but it was locked;
no services today.
I tried the town hall,
but it was closed
for the bank holiday.
Finally I went to the
shopping centre, but
there were only shoppers,
and if God had been there
they hadn't noticed.
I wandered home that
evening, through the slow light.
I took off my best clothes,
my finest shoes and
came down to supper.
My family asked if I had
seen God; sighing I shook
my head. One by one
they kissed my disconsolate
brow and smiled.
That night I dreamed
I met a God who kissed
my brow and smiled.

# Walking with My Wife

Walking in the woods with you,
voicing the gist and glint of our hopes.
Frost riming, white glazing branches
drooping towards the dark river's pitch.
What will trick the secret shadows
to make a revelation of themselves?
How can we lay bare sunlit gold
and not be scorched by incandescence?
The years and season's passing have
never palled the chance to embark,
to instigate our interlacing love,
the slender strands of our well-spun web,
the befriending of our broken souls,
and beckon the magic this walk extols.

# The Call of the Unwritten

'time would take me up to the swallow thronged loft' *Dylan Thomas*

A feathery uncertainty
in the swallow-thronged loft,
I am tongue-tied in a company
of singers, these fleet poets of the air.
Yet well fed and ready for flight,
I tremble on the claw-pocked ledge
and wait. Wait for my turn to squeeze
through the tiny round chance
that leads to the sky.
Never before has the call felt
so inexorably feral nor the wind so
giddy. Then the instinctual draw rises
in my feather-bound chest,
and I burst out of the loft
like an arrow at a target, though
no target I have ever seen. Sweeter
than the nectar of the honeysuckle
is this jubilation of flight. Suicidal
to the praise-seeking self that kept me
loft bound in constant comparison
to finer feathers. Can I trust my
inner compass and continue this
migratory flight to a rewritten me?
Can I accept the unnamed future
whispering in fragile beating wings?
A flight that captures the fierce jeopardy
of living so I can render its path for
others to read, a slow crossing to an
undisclosed country, with a chorus
of chanters to the southern sun. In
this throng I have found my voice, and
besides the loft is behind me now.

# The Relics of Saint Therese

Your little bones have travelled far
from your monastery in Normandy,
which you vowed never to leave.
A radio presenter asked me, is this
not superstition, people venerating bones?
I said perhaps, but then it is
an ancient instinct to try and touch
divinity in the body. There
are holy wells throughout the land
where we brought babies
for the blessing of the goddess. One
outraged man sent a letter and
holy pictures of the modest saint to remind
me of my faith. But Therese knew and I know
that Jesus did not wear a little golden
button that said Roman Catholic on it.
He carried a tender heart that said
a freeing word gifts an infinite horizon,
a single moment so dazzling that
no eye can hold it, a surge of
mercy that encircles rapture and
despair, and that walking with
small steps towards the speechless
wonder cannot be carried in a
golden box or contained in any church;
it is the offer of every human dawn.
I hope your bones speak as loud as your life.

Written on the occasion of the visit of the relics of Saint Thérèse of Lisieux to Sheffield, 8 October 2009.

# Jung Said

Jung said
that every part
of a dream
is a part of the
dreamer
aching for
reunion.
In the collective
dream that
we call Jesus,
what violence
has it taken
to make him
disappear
into the shadows,
and what part
of ourselves
would
rise up
if,
as in the story,
he came back?

# Emmaus

Take a long unhurried walk
with a willing other,

keep a measured silence as your four
feet trudge the miles,

honour the sparse and common space
that shrewdly shapes between you,

narrate in quietness the chronicle of your living
with all its broken light,

do not spare the brittle self in your
honestly forming story,

nor judge the wounded self that wants
to nestle in your arms,

or any of the legion selves that emerge
as you summon them,

be gentle with your broken hopes
and kind to your successes,

with respect hear the restive steps
of this re-collecting journey,

recognize the natural, animate around you
life echoing your own,

then breach the generosity of solitude
with a welcome to the wanderer,

take turns in pathway sharing, break
out your spoken story,

be heedful as a deep-barked forest
to every breaking twig,

frame each exposure with the
intentness of a lens,

stop and face each other with a
bold unwavering gaze,

see the walking miles reflected
in the pupil of the other,

and by embracing what remains, you
will have reached Emmaus.

**Emmaus**: an ancient town seven miles North West of Jerusalem – *Wikipedia*

# An Unexpected Passion

You walked into the glare
of the lights with three crosses
hanging over your head, like
someone awaiting Calvary. The
judges barely suppressed
their sneers as the chief asked
you to speak. To voice your
bold ambition to be a singer,
which caused the crowd to
caterwaul and scoff. The caption
below your head read Susan
Boyle, unemployed, forty-seven,
as you opted to perform a
dream instead of speaking of it.

The opening bars swept
over the jaded, cynical faces
of judges and mob alike, joined
in the dark thrill of ridicule.

You opened your mouth and
a voice of rapture burst from
your stout Scottish frame,
a voice hitherto saved for
a mother who died and a
small front room in Bathgate.

Mouths opened, eyebrows
raised, cheers rent the darkness,
the tide of mockery turned in
an instant. 'I had a dream my life
would be so different from the

hell I'm living.' The bleakness
of years of isolation altered
when a finger pressed play.

Thirty-three million times to
date, this moment has been
viewed on the small screen,
the power of the human dream
peeping out from under bushy
eyebrows. We saw our ugly duckling
awkwardness, smoothed to a
swan's grace yet carried in the
same body. She still carries her
wounds for all to view, and she didn't
win the show. But she did a
thing we all recognise: she rose
from the dead before our eyes.

# Song of a Motherless Son

I went to Assisi to recall my mother
one year after her lonely cross,
a need to evade sorrow's smother
one year after my searing loss.
Carrying grief in my unwashed hair,
I came at night to the Umbrian plain.
The city of peace was glowing there,
a gleam of mercy through a squall of pain.

I trod the steps of Francis's feet
and only went where I was led.
To open my soul I did not eat
but trudged uphill with an aching head.
There I found his weathered figure,
a bronze homage to holy rest,
body unfolded in tranquil stature
gazing into the summoning west.

I carried a box of silver sorrow,
the cremation of her time-worn days;
around his head an ashy halo
a symbol of my dismal haze.
The shock of loss was still my psalm,
as I had reached the end of tether;
an open window the evening's balm
as I laid myself on a bed of weather.

So I said to myself if I should wake;
the saint's day mass I would take.

Dawn's soft dimness greeted my feet
in the narrow pink-stoned street.
Spidery movement on pavement cobble

bending me low to broken hobble.
Glancing upward I found its source:
a white shone feather's downward course.
I raised and opened my left hand;
it landed like water on hard baked sand.
I felt like one who is singled out,
chosen as broken, a man of doubt.
I curled my hand around its grace;
it touched my soul like a mother's face.
In the darkened crypt of the barefoot saint
I knelt as tears washed away constraint.
The trauma died as they broke the bread,
and wine woke a mother to stand in her stead.

# The Boy Within

I am caught between a
future that age is prising
from my weakening hands
and a past that recruits
regrets to stand for my
missed chances. Chances
that slipped by as I was
busy proving my self.

My present is so much
less enticing than when I was
twenty, even on holiday
there I am waiting for myself.

Unbidden I recall a photo
of my junior school face,
his boyhood clad in a mother
knitted jumper and a smile.
Blondness beams out at me,
as I sense his presence down
near my spine, rising from
unmined depths. With it comes
a memory of my boy as he
throws sticks at the great
horse chestnut, dislodging a
spiky green orb. His new fingers
split the skin to reveal a russet
grained conker in white flesh.

This tender opening reweaves
me with myself, as I stand now
in my fiftieth year, with comfortable

girth and prescription for blood
pressure tablets. Flourishing again
the boy steps through this
unremembered gate; taking
my hand, pulling me through
as his smile lifts the
wrinkles from my frown.

All these years I have been trying
to grow up into a settled man,
but suddenly I want to grow down
into rescued innocence.

# Brief Beauty

The jasmine that flowers in my
January house owns just one
short day of pristine whiteness
and of course the perfume of
rapture. It is the same with
the frost, when I open my door
to the dawn and stare at the
laced leafed whirls, presented
like a chill blooded artist's
opening show. Works achieved
in temperatures below freezing,
these crafty etches are gone
when the sun rising over the
naked sycamores kills them.

In this tiny margin of days, if I
upturn the reckless snowdrops
like a jeweler valuing diamonds,
I see a vision of miniature
elegance in doll's house green
and yellow. But the shortest
of days frequently slip by whilst
I remain in the cautious warmth,
futilely busy with things urgent
but of no importance. Whilst
outside nature offers such
unprolonged grace, to be seen
again only after a year's turning.

I gaze at the early setting sun and
wonder whether I will return
with the frost and the flowers

and the blissful scent to savour
such beauty in brevity. Whether
or not I do, in this elegy, the
fleeting brilliance will still gleam
ephemerally through, and perhaps
this brief beauty will transform me.

# Disconsolation

October is such an untidy month;
the leaves fall quicker than I can
sweep them, and my gutters are
crammed with their moldy corpses.

The mizzle the wind spills over
the eve's edge makes the stones
of my home clammy. The clocks
have made their yearly march
back to winter quarters, and the
dogs' paws mark a muddy muddle
on my kitchen floor. It is a time for
writing, for decanting the juices
that have fermented all summer.

But I am so distressed by the length
of each night and the bleak looks the
leaf dropping beeches give me when I
pass them in the valley, that I fear to sit
at my table and face the vacuity of the page.

I feel so personally the inborn
demise confided to me by the
dying wasp or the departing swallow;
that I can only write the grubby cantos
of autumn bonfires, whose smoke
curls and fades in the misty air.
These wisps of disconsolation
are a fleeting eulogy to falling,
a carol to the withering season.

# Last Rites

When I am gone,
take up your kitchen broom,
sweep three stars down
from the cobwebbed sky.

Place the first in my coffin;
its bleach-bright light
will suffuse my guttered flame,
waken life's soiled toil
to the tear-dried home,
prepared.

Place the second
in my tended garden,
where my gardener
will look for me,
where it started.

Place the last on a chain
around your neck;
wear it as a sacrament
of the lights we kindled.

Then when the stars
tumble from the sky
at the end, our shining
will illuminate scars on
love's invincible face.

# The Chair Maker Cycle

## i

# Absence

I am a chair maker
to one who left;
there is the empty seat,
with its Deus absconditus smirk.
Of course chairs have no faces,
yet even as my back turns
and weeks pass, the chair grins.
I could sit in it, but I prepared it
for a well-met God
when I was a carver's apprentice,
a memorial to the
one who sat for a while, then rose,
giving no reason for going.
I wonder if it splintered?
But I sanded every edge,
my fingers bled, the timber darkened,
and now leaving is written in the
story of the knotted wood.
Better to carve than have redundant hands?
You would think so but pain cuts to the quick,
my eyes sting with staring,
the chair keeps grinning,
and I am scared to stop.
I pay out my days in a cruel carpentry,
a house full of chairs to see if they grin too.

## ii
# Exhaustion

In this house full of chairs
I am at the end of myself,
needing relief from this barren labour.
Yet I cannot shift the sense
that a dark magic is in me,
a malignant source of loss
that summoned death into my life.
Like a contagious man who
infects others but not himself,
I dare not get close for fear of loss.
So I am lonely in the house of Job,
stumbling around, crashing through
rooms full of seats, as now I have
admitted these faithless counselors
who usurp the carven seats of God.
My comfortless comforters declare me
'a man of glass chipping at every turn',
'a man of ice melting in the sun',
'a man of sores, wounds that will not heal'.
I hate my analysts, with their sure-fire
belief in meaninglessness.
So I lay the broken child of my body
on the driftwood floor
and crumple into the arms of sleep.

## iii

# Wreckage

Sleep is a healer, but mine is ravaged
by dreams of blame, refrains of disdain,
adding to the atheists' accusative prose.
I am at a loss, waking or sleeping;
even the world of dreams cannot
unhorn my dilemma. In both
I stand before the enlightened court
of science declaring an end to
God, a triumph of easy certainty,
the sovereignty of reason.
Their verdict on me that chair
making equals a twisted act of faith.
Let it go, you will feel better, they
pronounce. Dreaming ends, I rouse to a
silent house, and I am left with
a misshapen paradox:
either divinity dreams of death
or God is Nietzsche's fatality,
and we live in an ungiven world.
I seize a hammer, smash the chairs,
an implosion of splinters; I sag down.
In that stillness I admit the lacuna of death,
Mother's cold body on her kitchen floor,
ashes of my father over summer graves.
But I know I saw you sitting
in that contented time,
so I cling to the wreckage of your chair,
caressing the spindles of doubt.

# iv
# Presence

A sound splits the speechless air
as the wood of my door is knuckle rapped.
I am worn with the smug atheists;
nonetheless I rise to go and open.
'Are you the chair maker?' The questioner
is brown of hair, clothes and skin,
weather born and threadbare with
long worn much-travelled boots.
Dusty, dusky face with dark pupiled
eyes in deep sockets of sight.
The figure enters as I step back.
I observe dirty bandages on hands
extended in self-presentation.
'Who are you?' I ask.
'I am legion, and you called me.
I am your death, the stark truth
of ended life; I am all death.
I am every life, grain seeded, star bursting.
I am the leviathans' swallow and I am swallowed.
I have the mark of Abel on me and blisters
from the fires of loss. I wept at the fall of
Sodom and the tomb of Lazarus. I
lace sweetness in a moment and
sweat in the heats of passion; my
passing is the song of cemeteries and
folded grave clothes. I am heaven's bending
hell's mending, the glistening tear streak
of a mother's grief. In all that is I am.
I am no chair sitter, and we need to leave.

'Art has two constant unending preoccupations: it is always meditating upon death and it is always thereby creating life.'

*Doctor Zhivago* by Boris Pasternak

# Inconsequence and Silence

We keep the radio
on in the kitchen
to keep the dogs
company, but perhaps
the underlying aim
is that by listening to
one world coming
through the digital signal
we can keep another
at bay. But if I go out
of the door and into
the garden, there is
an acre of silence
that makes all the
words in the kitchen
inconsequential.

# There Is One Thing Necessary

There is one thing necessary for life:
to take a single conscious breath
every day.

To fill the lungs with an inhalation
decreed by the mind,
assented by the heart,
and executed by the body

In that one breath, be a litany of nature.
Be the soaring of migrating swifts and
the gaze of the watchful heron on the meagre
branch. Be the unavoidable heartache of
the falling leaves announcing autumn.
Be the appearing of the rainbow on the
leading edge of a storm which
transmutes the season, darkening
into winter. Be the panic-laden
snow flurry that stops a city in its tracks.
Be the priestly cold of a frost-sketched
morning; be the celebrant of hard winter's
darkness; be the pitch-black swirl
of snow melting water as it runs over
river-bound, lichen-clad rocks. Be the call of the
owl hunting in the dimness of the wind
rustled copse. Be the grey-garbed land tinged
with the waxen ashes of freezing fog. Be the first
indomitable heads of snowdrops squeezing
through a hard-rimed soil. Be the energy of
infusing spring whose sudden green is fire.
Be the so-called bind weed that produces
the free white trumpet of the morning
glory nodding in a summer breeze.

Be inspiration
and expiration.

Be the life that is yours alone,
a unique moment
of breathing revelation
and a stark reminder
to all life
that you can take one breath
that holds the turning world.

There is one thing necessary for life:
to take a single conscious breath
every day, and then to take another.

# Gabriel

There is a thud as
my dog Gabriel
rises up from the
ground and lumbers
his front paws on to
the arm of my chair.
He leans his face
into mine. His bullet
headed friendship
and tenacious fondness
triumph over me;
at once I drop
whatever I am doing
to pat him.

Border black
and white, with brown
eyes in my blue ones,
and in his coat
the lonely aroma
of the sheep-filled hills.
My monochrome friend,
my running comrade,
my core rendered
in animal form.
His prone body,
down now,
next to my feet,
his panting warmth
on my toes,
his breathing
punctuated with hefty
sighs as he dreams.

The language
of his paws
on the ground
of my heart,
addresses me
from the green
world, the gentle
nature that pays
the price of my living,
begging me to listen.

# The Raven-Haired Woman

Fresh-faced raindrops clung to me as through
childhood's doorway to the teenage party I came,
laden with homemade sherry and cheap cigarettes.
The hallway awash with shoes, keeping the good carpets
clean. In through the huddling adolescent darkness
she led me by the hand to the sofa, hers
by dint of it being the house she grew up in.
My stomach went smooth, like running silk,
not knowing how to kiss. Yet she kissed me,
her lips parting over my thin, milky teeth.
We separated like ghosts and spoke no more of it
as I returned her to her pedestal.

When we met again, she was Cheri not Susan,
and her glasses enlarged the darkness of her eyes.
A short journey brought her a long way,
from her parents' tenancy to our flat with service charges.
She was curvy, it was hypnotising, our kisses
promised more – but she left me at the bus stop.

Later on in the seventies, in my bedroom with the orange
plastic light, on an old set, I saw the *Summer of '42*.
Desire stirred in me again as the older woman educated
the boy.

Eighteenth birthday, my mother brewed grief now not
sherry, as I left the legal pub with two golden girls.
In their parentless house we lay, all three together,
enwrapped and raptured. I was golden, in the arms of
the adored,
their gilded bodies my boon, cooing and laughing in the
dark.

My clumsiness did not know how to touch them as
they descended to my floor, but when I explored
them, their breath quickened and their eyes shone.
Small caresses only; my bungling boyhood deferred
our coming together, unspent but heavenly,
a confluence of the raven-haired woman and me.

But she helped me grow toward the man I am, as
I see her now in these words I write, in wifely eyes,
the daughter of my memory, the desire of my soul.
And still I long for the raven-haired muse at night.

# The Circles of Women

Last evening I found myself
in a circle of women,
whose children
had slipped under the
slick surface of addiction.
Proud women, women in pain,
working women with
helpless husbands,
unable to dry their tears.

It took me to a time
when I worked in a circle
of young women,
prams full of kids, pop
and crisps. Outside the
Miners Welfare they
showed me a playground,
cracked tarmac under
broken swings, strewn
with dreadful diamonds;
smashed bottled glass
tearing into their children's feet.

I taught them to speak
from their own throats,
to organise in
the council rooms,
the smoking town halls
of condescending men.
They found their voices and
stood tall in their village.
Fixing their ruined streets,
they began to mend their lives.

Last night was a sterner test;
we found ourselves in a
darkened wood, and the
path ran out. Their sons
had entered the forest at
the blackest point and
been taken by the
oily fingers of narcosis. These
women had followed them
into the dark and I had
to show that the blackness
between the trees had
grace to heal. To tell them
the tracks that lined the
arms of their offspring
were not the end of the
road. To perform rituals
of loss and rites of hope
right there in the gloom.
The lost children in the
invisible world slowly
gathered around to be
scolded, to feel the vicious
heat of their mothers' aching,
to hear the voice of love
once more and whisper into
cradling arms to let me go.

I asked them to drop
a black pebble of loss
into the salty well of
grief. Then one day

to draw from that same
well of relinquished anguish
a white stone of life
naming them wounded
yet intact, but only when
its time. Until then I know
I will return to the wood
and sit in the circle
of red-eyed women
to speak with them
of the nature of healing
in the washing of tears.

# The Rook and the Hawk

Driving up the steep hill past the farm,
on the road to school with my son.
We watch a rook; wind buffeted,
he spreads his fingering wings; the
broad, black gloves of an undertaker as
he settles on an oak's aging branch.
The wintry sun narrows our eyes
as we see the tree's shadow, skeletal
bronchioles abandoned by their leaves.
My twelve-year-old boy, the light
in his face squinting and sneezing,
catches sight of a hawk standing still
above us, until it closes its feathered
arms and plummets, a skewering arrow.
'It's catching rodents in the grass,' I say.
'It must have amazing eyesight,' he replies.
Present to the presents of life, the boy;
prescient to the presence of death, the man.

# Frontier Dream

*'I always wanted to see the frontier before it's gone.'*
  Lieutenant John Dunbar, *Dances With Wolves*

I dreamed
of a dance floor
in the colonial tropics,
its veneered smoothness
full of holes, like wounds.
At the ragged edge of each,
a rotting thatch over dark
waters, overarched by
an ornate glasshouse
stilted into the swamp.

Through this
colonial outpost
I move from gash to gash
as a strange woman
glides towards me. She is
unsolved and handsome,
painted with dark totems.
Her black pupils summon
me to abandon this festering
outpost I once thought
the greatest of adventures.

She leads
me to her tribal lands
where she embraces my
whiteness with her brownness.
What could I possibly
offer her with my weapons
and rapacious capacity
for jungle destruction?

She draws me into her
lips, kisses the fragility
she finds there, strips me
of my defences and asks
me to defend her.

I go
with her deep into
the forest where she stoops
to draw in the soil, teaching
the runes and rituals of
living and dying. She kindles
the fire of yearning with the
sparks of loneliness
and tells me to stay in solitude
for a year and a day.

Only
when I have sunk deep
into the rich soil of silence
does she come to unearth me.
I am wasted and wind born;
she washes me in the river of
her belonging and caresses my
courage out of its trembling cage.
We perform the marriage of
kindness and garland each other
with flowers from the poison ivy.
Her sari is golden, and I wear
a single white robe; we part
the river of death.

In my dream
I live with her way
beyond the frontier. I
know the ways of the imperial
forces, and I teach her to
avoid them. She in her turn
teaches me the sacraments
of earth and paints my body
with the patterns of the Jaguar.
I forget what shoes are for.

Occasionally
I return to the colony
to observe the habits of
progress, absurd to me now.
The glasshouse is ruined,
the rainforest claimed it.
Once in a while I sing
the songs of the frontier
to any who will come to the
edge and listen.

When I awoke
from the dream, I began to
envision it into my life.

# The Pillowed State

Pensively struggling with my difference from you,
my huddled foetal partner, rolled up and over.
My colourful creature of discomfort, do you need
my reassurance as I am scared to touch in the dark?

Eat with me, speak and be spoken to
over dates and Kasbah cocktails.
Cover me with your nightgowns,
come back to the pillowed state.
Crease yourself, let staples mark you,
volumise you, be encyclopaedic, be drawn.

Your isolation pains me, so inside your cocoon.
Chrysalised, you never come forth, character of
incommunicado. You are a caravan on the desert trail,
coursing but never arriving. Come in, come home.

The spectre of your hidden self haunts me;
I met you in a side street souk, dark-skinned,
weathered, untethered and Mecca like. The wind
caught your sails, and you were billowed, winnowed
by Krishna. Come to me, true you, and pour
into my well; be fulsome, be overflowing, be loved.

# What My Migraines Taught Me

They always start
with a pinking sheared
flash across my vision.
Then a numbness
in the fingers and the feet.
My speech is next,
as if my words
are jigsaw pieces and
none of them will fit.

I have to lay down,
the last to go
are my thoughts; nothing
makes sense.
But that is the
startling thing: there
is still a me, beyond
sense, beyond mood,
beyond scrutiny.

Like Aragorn sitting
in the corner of a
crowded inn or the
sound of Gandalf's staff on
the round green door
of my interrupted life.

At first I was scared
that my migraines
would trap me unawares
in the middle of the
traffic of my life.

But now I know
they introduced
me to the stranger
that is my soul,
and he is there
with his travel
stained boots,
guiding me.

Waiting for me
to ask him
where to now?

# A Poem for My Children

I am not sure how well
I fathered you; only
you can tell, and I
am scared to ask.

As your grew
we played the hide
and seek of spring,
tucking you to bed
I glimpsed gloom
and glow in your dreams,
and we voyaged the seas
of juvenescence that
are always sailed before
the maps can be made.

At Christmas I was
Santa, you mistook
me for the crimson king,
kissing me with innocent
lips, eyes shining before
the Herod of adulthood
carried off your infancy.

I waged the grown-up war
only to make you the casualties.
For that and many other failings
as a father, *je suis désolé*.

In recompense and to offset
my faults, I want you to
know how the world has
made itself known to me.

Life will not present itself
to you like low-hanging
fruit in easy orchards.
Sadly others will get
the applause as you stand
in the wings and watch,
but trust me, plaudits
are a masquerade.

Your life is within,
a fine filament
that arises in your
given soul. This is the
place the great tales
speak of; where
the tenderness of your
regrets will beckon
to a desperate crossing
and a dark doorway.

Then you,
like Theseus,
will find that to face a
minotaur you follow
that glimmering strand
to the wounded bird
of your vulnerability
laying between his
subtle hooves.

In that meeting
the monster will
be your teacher,
unveiling in you
the unquenchable
font of life.

Then you will never
have to ask a stranger
to tell you who you are;
you will have stepped
onto your spot-lit mark,
and the soft memory
of my voice will
be your prompt.

# Warts of Wisdom

For two years now I have
had a wart on my right foot.
My doctor was surprised;
this type, he commented,
usually appeared on elderly men.
Too much best foot forward
has aged me before my time.

He employed nitrous oxide
to scour it from my skin; with
a blast of searing scorch he
whitened and further wizened
the wart. As weeks passed the
crust peeled away to reveal
the self-same growth, persistent
as midges in a Scottish bog.
Is this wart the wintered part
of me, the hidden effect of
the anxiety of this overloaded
world, an outcrop of elderliness
anxiously asking to be heard?

Witches earned the cronish
warts of wisdom by permitting
life's raging blasts to enter
them, to alter their innards.
I want to learn from my wart
the insight held in a risk-ridden
roaming that matures me like
a ruby merlot or a bronzed single
malt. I will not bury the pain of
living so that it all erupts one day,
fiercely in a deluge of trouble.

# The Curriculum of Winter

My journey home is through an aisle of beeches
flowing cathedrally regal in twilit gleaming;
strong branches form natural cloistered reaches
grey gathered arches of patinated pearling.

My lights illumine an aisle of restitution, a palace
for the earthy crowning of my inborn nature,
I glimpse between the trunks a sad and pallid face
of the white winter horse standing solemn yet unsure.

His skittish gallop mimics a free plain's ranging.
Horses were once unbound, not framed
into our lives; we stole their freedom, caging
a cheerless bondage in which all are tamed.

A place where feeling is traded for control, flinging
billions at reckless banks, gilded confetti over a
hapless marriage that will cost us all, quibbling
over cuts, anything to elude the curriculum of winter.

But America's addicts know that recovery is a twelve
step process in whose freezing season we can divine
the darkness, strip the ego like bark off the birch, and delve
into the hidden marrow where night and light entwine.

The winter horse and the twilight journey tell of vows
we need to make in the beeches cathedral, confessing
impotence, a first step of weakness, to arouse
the power that disarms the soul to suffer nature's blessing.

# The Real Truth

To be truthful
I don't always
know what life is
for. Yes, there
are sparks of clarity
in the stubble of
the commonplace.

But most days I live in
a cloudy unknowing.
Disorientated,
just negotiating
the next task, without
becoming the opposite
of the early dawn
stillness I long to
embody.

Of course I
have read many baggy
handbooks on the need
to be present to my life,
to God or even to my dog.

Once or twice in a
month of mornings
I touch something,
and out of insight's
grain store garnered
(from the wise ones)
comes winnowing out
an ear of wisdom.

Telling me that
my soul is a
cast and ringing
bowl, that if I
stay still long enough,
my soul will show up
like an image through
tracing paper.

I wonder
though (the wise ones),
do they really do it,
or are they, like me,
fleetingly conscious,
that it might be
true?

And have they like me,
wished all the shadows,
cast by previous stabs
at contact, would move out
of the way?

But perhaps the real truth
is; that the shadows are
it, and we just haven't
realised they are the
presence in disguise.

# The Needle on the Don

## i

The needle's eye blinks through the rain.
Falling now, falling yesterday, long before
its needling made a pointly finger
in the parting beeches standing round.
Once the cloud's scalded tears swelled
the Don, stung by the great blasting
furnaces of Atlas, the steel world on
his shoulders. The smelters are melted
now, gone the way of all iron to the
scrapping merchants in their rusted lands.
The Don streams on, the only sign of
a steelworked past, the fig trees sprouting
from excreted seeds. Germinated in Vulcan's
steaming urine that gushed in heated torrents
to foul and warm the sweet waters of Rivelin
and Sheaf. The fig bears no fruit now,
and its leaves cannot cover our trespasses.
But we are still Danu's children, not the Cossacks
she mothered in Russia, where the Don
quietly flows. Not Danube's azured offspring as
her balm heals the lands of once war-torn Europe.
We are the grime-stained survivors from
a blasted city, our industrial Gods culled
as the deicidal iron lady rode north.
But Danu is older than false Boudicca
and has rusted her callous chariot.
Now we must go to the birthing Pennines
whose springs are a cradle of kindering.
To be born of her crucibling womb, cast in
her image, flowing stoically to the disused
anthracite plains, carrying our lost to the sea.
Her mothering is not craven like London's
towering ravens, whose panaceas are call centres.
Reaping revenue from retail replicas and
streets that look the same from Pittsburgh to
Pitsmoor. The needle blinks on through the rain.

## ii

The blinking eye sees all.
Litter and rough sleepers, cider bottles,
cheek by jowl to pavestone pilgrims
bound for the meadow's hall.
A cathedral in green cupolas,
man hand made it, we consume it.
What the needle's gaze sees is that
we have unsighted ourselves, we are blind;
great Vulcan and Atlas are eyeless in Brightside.
No seeing child will lead them temple wise
to put their Samson backs against
the false pillars of mammon and push.
Instead Danu's children pour into the basilic maw
to the glittering plenitude of the horns of making.
The worship of these goods mars and scars them,
each homecoming a fruitless consummation.
The speakers blare muzak and messages
declaring us all rich now – rich in credit,
rich in debt, rich in things but not in living.
Downriver, the brambling of ruined houses,
electricity off, disconnected and sealed shut.
Where flowers grew in wide estates
riders have no joy, burnt out in scorched abandon.
The needle's eye blinks on the rain-washed
wilderness, a silent invitation to another path.
Make the smooth places rough, the high places low;
callous up the fleshy hand with the labour
of another birth. The work of handholding
through the dark, of candle making with local
tallow, of carving with peaks of stone a new
city for Danu's children. A place of creating
and not consuming, of the commerce of our characters,
not our goods. Of a life assayed and hallmarked
made in Sheffield, a dream of steel and stature.
The river's arms are full of divining
compassion that nurtures our dignity
and fashions a freeing cast to our steel.
The shoppers return on bus and tram;
when the shopping is done, what then?

A city of steel but no alloy,
can we heat the crucible again?
The needle's eye blinks on the Don,
But who will pass through it?

Written after seeing the sculpture *The Eye of the Needle* by David Nash on the bank of the River Don near Meadowhall in Sheffield. The Don derives its name from Dôn (or Danu), a Celtic mother goddess

# No Such Thing as Right or Wrong

There is no such thing
as right or wrong,
good or bad;
only wounds after blows,
and then with an
allowing that forgives a
long walk to freedom.

You may want to cling
to black and white,
but beware the ready
stone that comes to
hand when the sin is
not your own. Remember
in Eve's blunder and
Adam's stumble the
proscribed fruit cursed
an awareness of bareness,
self-justifying in the seeds
and the flesh. That once
eaten harvest forced them
to huddle in the jungle, hiding
from a gloaming breeze that
longed to complete them.

If you become judge and
jury, split off from the
vast approval, you will find
an innocent paradise
barred to you and know
every day that the choice
has been yours.

But if you can vow
with the Bodhisattvas
to be a Jesus, to save
all breathing beings;
if you can rule out
right or wrong, good
or bad, see the world
as it is and forgive it;
then you will find a
sword raising within
to unveil an opening,
and as you walk in
that garden clutching
your cracked spirit,
you will touch the gentle
face of a tender evening.

# The Georgia O'Keefe Museum

'Abba Poeman said "If Moses had not led his sheep to Midian he would have seen him who was in the bush."' *The Sayings of the Desert Fathers*

## i

I gaze at the painting
of a bleached sheep's skull,
ivory smooth against a cobalt
sky. Squinting bright sunlight
spills over the crumbled
edges of yellow sandstone.
Fluid warmth seeps into the
pink midline and then down
into the blood-stained
groin of the cliff, knee
deep in crimson rubble.

A scorched landscape
rivuleted by rare rain.
The caption by the
painting reads that Georgia
O'Keefe painted and
dwelt at Ghost Ranch.
Legend names it the place
of the hanged man, and
I am caught suspended
as I look uneasily on
her tear-chiselled canyons.
The early sun rises over
the bones of the rocks,
revealing the dark vaginal
shadows that obliged her
to sing of calla lilies
and furtive purple irises.

## ii

Seven years ago,
for one such sun's
initiatory pass I drew
in the desert's glower
a man-sized shaman's circle.

There at the ranch of ghosts,
I faced the Pedernal,
the footstool that God
promised the artist that
if she painted it enough,
he would donate it to her cause.

An aboriginal mountain
sacred to the painted natives,
a place of flint sharded
stones, good for arrowheads,
a jagged ground on which to
walk unshod. My back that day
against an ancient monolith
standing seven stone feet
into the desert's breath.
Hard, erect and generative,
but I, the flaccid man, wilted
in the solar kiln and had
to surrender to my firing.

I learned from the shaman's
circle that we all need daily
deaths to augur its fullness.

## iii

In the artist-framed
morning nothing stirs
yet all is shimmering.
Georgia told me the dead
of the desert are more
alive than the city
scraped skies with
their callous critics.

She fled with her lover from the
self-confident columnists;
she favoured the dealings
of diamond-backed rattlesnakes.

From her photograph,
the artist turns to me
astride an ancient Indian
motorbike; tanned hands
grip tightly a man's back.
A man who is to take her
out past Kitchen Mesa
into untamed territory,
an undiscovered country
of deep-starred stillness.

I yearn to go after those
Muse-filled eyes and iris
stained hands.

## iv

But I am afraid that
this painted desert will
disclose my oldest fear that
I am of no consequence.
Her pictures render the
fierce inner landscape
whose heat causes my
wavering truth to cloy
in my parched mouth.
How do I find a voice
in this ferocious emptiness?

Yet she did it, this
brown, prune-wrinkled
artist on whose work I
gaze with such envy.

She gave birth to art
in a blazing wilderness,
as from another painting a
scorpion wields his fatal
tail; is it summoning me?
Is it to me that the
snake shaman rattles?

Who can say, but I am going
anyway, leaving to meet
a stripped God hidden
in a flaming pinion tree.
Leaving to raise bone-smooth
poems, to send back words
born of the desert, to die
so many deaths that the
last will not be the end but
an entrance into naked life.

Summer 2009 Santa Fe, New Mexico

# ACKNOWLEDGEMENTS

Loving thanks to:
My wife Wilma, for her constancy,
My three children, Eva, Lara, and Tom; critics and friends,
Mark Pickin for days of sharing, a better man than me,
Daniel O'Leary for paternity in the mystery of writing,
Belden Lane for the solace of fierce landscapes and mirroring my best self back to me,
David Whyte for a wonderful Salon Series that opened a door,
All those on the Salon for the circle of vulnerability,
All at RODA (Relatives of Drug Abusers – Sheffield) for allowing me to touch a painful world,
Stephen Gambill for pushing me further,
Stephen Picha for brotherhood,
Richard Rohr (*ofm*) for vision,
My Sheffield Men's Circle, whose honesty is wealth,
All those I listen to, for companionship and for trusting me,
My lovely mother, who always wanted to see a book with my name on it,
The Rivelin Valley that cradles me.

Quote from Sweet Darkness by David Whyte is to be found in *River Flow: New and Selected Poems 1984–2007* printed with permission from Many Rivers Press, www.davidwhyte.com. ©Many Rivers Press, Langley, Washington.